CW01496979

Original title:
Bubbling Duns Across the Elf Park

Copyright © 2025 Swan Charm

Author: Paulina Pähkel
ISBN HARDBACK: 978-1-80563-270-2
ISBN PAPERBACK: 978-1-80564-791-1

Celestial Fables in the Forest's Heart

In the forest deep and wide,
Stars whisper secrets, softly guide.
Fables dance on moonlit leaves,
Bringing dreams and tales that weave.

Creatures gather, wise and old,
Sharing stories yet untold.
The nightingale sings a sweet tune,
Underneath the silver moon.

With every rustle, shadows play,
In dappled light where fairies sway.
Each twig and stone holds a rhyme,
Echoing the pulse of time.

Wandering paths where echoes dwell,
Nature's magic weaves its spell.
A tapestry of light and shade,
In this enchanted glade.

So listen close when night is near,
For every sound is crystal clear.
With every breeze, you'll find your part,
In celestial fables, right from the heart.

Twinkling Trails by the Streamlet

By the stream where waters gleam,
Twinkling trails of a gentle dream.
Pebbles dance in rippling light,
Nature's wonders, pure delight.

Silver fish dart with grace,
Tracing circles in a chase.
Each splash a laugh, a fleeting thrill,
In the streamlet's crystal chill.

Dragonflies flit, their wings aglow,
Painting patterns where they go.
Rustling reeds whisper their cheer,
As the world melts into the clear.

Moonbeams twirl on water's skin,
Kissing currents where dreams begin.
Follow the path, let heart take wing,
For joy is found in every spring.

So linger here, let moments blend,
Where twinkling trails and time suspend.
Embrace the magic the stream bestows,
In waters calm, your spirit grows.

Rhapsody of Reflections and Glimpses

In the quiet pool, a story weaves,
Reflections dance amongst the leaves.
Glimpses of stars and tales of yore,
Whispered in ripples, forevermore.

The colors swirl, a painter's brush,
Mirroring dreams in a gentle hush.
Each moment caught, a fleeting glance,
In the stillness, dreams can enhance.

With every breath, the world unfurls,
A tapestry of wonders and swirls.
The heart finds rhythm, a vibrant beat,
In the soft embrace of time's retreat.

As shadows stretch and daylight fades,
Reflections grow in evening glades.
The rhapsody sings, a soothing song,
Of ephemeral beauty, where we belong.

So gaze within and feel the flow,
Of whispered dreams that softly glow.
In reflections deep, let your heart find,
The magic woven through the mind.

Playful Waters in the Whimsical Wild

In playful waters, laughter rings,
Where joyous heart and nature sings.
Meandering paths, a bubbly spree,
Come dip your toes, wild and free.

The brook frolics with a gleeful rush,
In laughter's current, feel the hush.
Each leaf a boat on a joyful ride,
As nature weaves the playful tide.

Sunbeams sprinkle in merry jests,
Winds swirl round like playful guests.
The world alive with joyous charms,
Enchanting hearts in nature's arms.

In splashes bright, the water glows,
Every ripple where magic flows.
A symphony of life, pure and bright,
In whimsical wilds, a sweet delight.

So dance by the stream, let laughter be,
In this playful realm of wild jubilee.
Where every splash and every cheer,
Engulfs your spirit, free as the deer.

The Laughter of Streams Underneath the Stars

Cold waters dance in glee,
Underneath the twinkling light,
Whispers brush the willow trees,
As night embraces dreams in flight.

The moon, a guardian bright,
Rests upon the rippling tide,
Guiding wishes with her sight,
While the world's troubles slide.

Crickets sing their lullaby,
Filling the air with gentle cheer,
Stars twinkle in the velvet sky,
Fleeting moments linger near.

Nature shares her ancient song,
Flowing soft like a poet's pen,
In this realm where hearts belong,
The laughter echoes once again.

So listen close, and you will hear,
The stories whispered from afar,
In the laughter of streams sincere,
Underneath the glowing stars.

Secrets Shared Under the Old Oak

Beneath the branches, wise and wide,
A gathering of hearts so true,
Whispers mingle, side by side,
In the shade, the dawning dew.

Laughter dances on the breeze,
As tales unfold in the light,
Memories nestled in the trees,
Guarded secrets, day and night.

The roots embrace the earth so dear,
Binding friendships, old and new,
With every laugh, a bloom appears,
In the warmth of a bond that grew.

Time spins slowly, like a thread,
Stitching moments here and there,
With every word, a story said,
In the shade, we have a prayer.

So gather close, beneath this oak,
Let the world drift far away,
For in this place, our hearts invoke,
The secrets shared, we shall not sway.

Whims of Light in the Emerald Hollow

In emerald glades where shadows play,
Light dances on leaves with delight,
Colors weave a bright ballet,
As whispers float into the night.

The sunbeams peek through canopies,
Painting patterns, soft and sweet,
Nature sings with gentle ease,
While fairies twirl on tiny feet.

Each beam a spark, a fleeting thought,
In the hollow's embrace, we roam,
Captured moments, never caught,
In this world, we find our home.

The breeze carries stories untold,
Of laughter shared in hidden spots,
A tale of wonders to behold,
Where time slips by, yet ne'er forgot.

So lose yourself in the emerald gleam,
And let your heart take to the sky,
For here, in magic's gentle stream,
The whims of light shall never die.

The Whispering Brook's Tale

A brook flows soft, with secrets rare,
Glistening pebbles, treasures unfold,
Whispers ride the cool night air,
In every ripple, stories told.

With each turn, a lesson learned,
Flowing forth from mountains high,
In the crook of time, we discerned,
The lessons written in the sigh.

Echoes of laughter blend with the song,
Of birds that flit in sunlight's grace,
In the brook, where we belong,
Time moves slow in this embrace.

As twilight deepens, tales take flight,
The brook's soft murmur calms the soul,
With every bubble, every light,
Nature's magic makes us whole.

So let the whispering waters draw,
You closer to their endless stream,
In the story of life, find awe,
And weave your dreams into the dream.

Echoing Lullabies of the Wildflowers

In fields where wildflowers sway,
Their whispers carry night and day.
With colors bright, they softly hum,
A lullaby to soothe the glum.

Beneath the sun's embracing glow,
They dance in breezes, all in tow.
Each petal holds a tale untold,
Of dreams and wishes, hearts of gold.

With dewdrops glistening like stars,
They keep the secrets of the spars.
Through fragrant scents on zephyrs ride,
The magic blooms, no need to hide.

As twilight drapes its velvet hue,
The wildflowers melt into the dew.
Their lullabies will ever stay,
To cradle night, to greet the day.

So wander through this vibrant land,
And let the lullabies expand.
For in each flower, life will sing,
Of hope and joy, and endless spring.

The Tinkle of Crystals in Misty Air

In forests deep where shadows play,
There lies a mist that swirls and sways.
With every breath, a crystal sound,
A melody that knows no bound.

Across the leaves, a gentle chime,
The tinkle echoes, lost in time.
Each droplet holds a secret bright,
A whisper soft, a spark of light.

As fairies dance on silken threads,
They weave the dreams that hope embeds.
With laughter ringing through the trees,
The crystal songs ride on the breeze.

With every heartbeat, feel the grace,
The world alive, a wondrous place.
In every tinkle, find a trace,
Of magic held in nature's embrace.

So wander forth where mist wraps tight,
And listen close to pure delight.
For in the air, the crystals sing,
A melody of every thing.

Secrets Shared by Gossamer Threads

In dawn's soft light, the spiders weave,
A tapestry of dreams to believe.
With gossamer threads, they softly spin,
The whispers of where magic begins.

Each delicate strand a story told,
Of secrets shared and mysteries bold.
In twilight's hush, they shimmer bright,
Connecting hearts like stars at night.

As breezes drift through wooded glens,
The threads will carry songs like pens.
They stitch together every hope,
In nature's craft, we find our scope.

With every glimmer, every shine,
A story waiting to be thine.
So listen close to the threads so fine,
For in their web, the world aligns.

So let your heart be drawn to see,
The gossamer paths where spirits flee.
For in each thread, a treasure lies,
A secret world beneath the skies.

The Play of Light upon Quiet Waters

Upon the lake where silence reigns,
The light dances, casting refrains.
With ripples that reflect the sun,
A play of shadows has begun.

In gentle waves that softly race,
The light finds beauty in each trace.
Like diamonds scattered on a dream,
Each glimmer plays, a gentle seam.

As evening falls and colors blend,
The waters whisper, journeys mend.
With every glint of sapphire blue,
The lake unveils its secrets true.

So let your spirit sail away,
On peaceful tides that softly sway.
For in the light, reflections bloom,
A quiet world that lifts the gloom.

So cast your gaze upon the stream,
Where every sparkle breathes a dream.
In quiet waters, hearts can roam,
And find within their truest home.

Whispers in the Enchanted Woods

In the hush of twilight's grace,
Leaves murmur secrets, soft and low,
Ancient trees, their wisdom trace,
Guard the tales that ebb and flow.

Moonlight dances, shadows play,
Foxgloves bloom with silver light,
Creatures stir and softly sway,
Bound by magic, lost from sight.

A whisper calls from deep within,
The unseen paths weave stories grand,
With every breath the night begins,
An eldritch world, at our command.

Mossy carpets, fragrant air,
Footsteps echo on the ground,
In this realm, a timeless affair,
Where lost and found are tightly bound.

Crickets sing, a symphony,
Stars awaken, twinkling bright,
Nature's heart beats endlessly,
In enchanted woods, heart takes flight.

The Murmuring Tides of Magic

Waves caress the moonlit shore,
Whispers weave through mist and foam,
In every tide, a mythic lore,
Ancient echoes call us home.

Shells that glimmer in the sun,
Harbor secrets of the deep,
Journeys dance as tides are spun,
Where dreams awaken from their sleep.

A lighthouse stands, its beacon bright,
Guiding souls through darkened night,
With every crash, a story told,
Of hidden realms and treasures bold.

Fortunes rise and fortunes fall,
Pirates sung in salty songs,
The ocean's voice, a siren's call,
A world where every heart belongs.

Underneath the starry dome,
Magic stirs with each tide's sweep,
In the swirling waves, we roam,
Murmuring dreams that never sleep.

Elfin Echoes in the Meadow

Beneath the boughs of whispering trees,
Where flowers wink at passing light,
Elfin laughter rides the breeze,
Spreading joy, a pure delight.

Golden sunlight bathes the glade,
Ferns and blossoms intertwined,
In this realm, no fear or shade,
Nature's song, enchantment combined.

Upon the hills, the soft winds sigh,
Carrying dreams on silky threads,
With every flutter, spirits fly,
Where ancient magic gently spreads.

Crisps of flowers, dew-kissed morn,
Every moment feels so rare,
In every heart, a hope reborn,
Elfin echoes fill the air.

So wander here where wonders weave,
And let your spirit hum and play,
For in this land, if you believe,
Elfin whispers guide your way.

Sprightly Streams and Sylvan Dreams

A brook doth babble, soft and clear,
Glistening under dappled light,
Sparkling water brings good cheer,
In sylvan realms, pure and bright.

Birch trees sway with gentle grace,
Whispers of the forest's heart,
In every shadow, a warm embrace,
Life and magic never part.

Leaves of gold that shimmer down,
Painting paths of purest green,
Nature spins her jeweled crown,
In splendor, we are truly seen.

Beneath the sun, we twirl and sway,
In the laps of nature's arms,
In every giggle, in every play,
Sprightly tales weave endless charms.

So let us dance upon the stream,
With sylvan dreams, our spirits soar,
In every flutter, a shared dream,
In harmony, forevermore.

Dreams Adrift on Spring Breezes

In fields where golden blossoms sway,
The whispers of the trees convey.
Beneath a sky of softest blue,
A world of dreams awaits for you.

With every breath, a fleeting sigh,
As petals dance, the moments fly.
The giggles of the young and free,
In spring's embrace, joy's symphony.

Chasing shadows, fleeting light,
In gentle warmth, the heart takes flight.
Through meadows lush, with hope we tread,
On fragrant paths where dreams are bred.

As twilight bends the day's refrain,
The stars emerge, a silver chain.
Each glowing orb, a whispered call,
To follow where the wishes fall.

So let the breezes guide your way,
With love and laughter on display.
For in this dance of springtime's art,
Our dreams, like flowers, bloom in heart.

Sylvan Serenades in Twilight Glow

In ancient woods where shadows play,
The twilight sings of end of day.
With rustling leaves and crickets' tune,
The forest hums beneath the moon.

Beneath the boughs, a secret place,
Where time stands still in nature's grace.
The whispers wrap like silken threads,
A lullaby for sleepy heads.

The owls, they wink with wise intent,
While fireflies dance, their magic sent.
Each melody, a tale retold,
Of dreams and wishes, bright and bold.

As moonbeams weave through branches high,
The stars awaken, dotting sky.
A serenade for souls that roam,
In twilight's embrace, we call it home.

So linger here, let worries part,
And find the music in your heart.
For every note, a moment's glee,
In sylvan spells, forever free.

Gems of Dew on Petals' Edge

At dawn's first light, the world aglow,
With diamonds twinkling soft and low.
Each dewdrop clings like whispered prayer,
On petals bright, so debonair.

In gardens lush where fragrances blend,
Nature's touch, a gentle friend.
The sun peeks in with golden grace,
To paint each flower's lovely face.

A dance of colors, vivid, rare,
Invites us in, as if to share.
The vibrant blooms, each tale unfolds,
A tapestry of life it holds.

As day ignites, the magic fades,
Yet beauty lingers in the glades.
For every gem that gently weeps,
A story waits, as daylight sleeps.

So cherish well this morning's art,
Each droplet like a tender heart.
In gardens where the dreams do wed,
The gems of dew on petals' edge.

Echoes of Mischief in Leafy Hideaways

In nooks and crannies, shadows play,
Where whispers hide and children stray.
With laughter sweet and secrets spun,
In leafy dens, the mischief's fun.

A squirrel darts with a cheeky grin,
While rabbits hop and softly spin.
The rustling leaves, a playful sound,
Where frolics and mischief abound.

The sunlight filters, a dappled dance,
Through branches bending, in pure romance.
Each hidden laugh, a tale to share,
In secret corners, magic's air.

With every breeze, a giggle flows,
As nature's heart, the wonder grows.
In leafy hideaways, dreams ignite,
A world of joy, both bold and bright.

So let your spirit roam away,
In whispered woods where fairies play.
For echoing tales of mischief's sway,
Craft memories that will never fray.

Symphony of Springs and Tales

In meadows green, where wishes bloom,
A symphony hums, dispelling gloom.
Each breeze a note, each flower a rhyme,
A tale of spring dances through time.

The brook sings soft, in murmurs sweet,
With laughter light and gentle beat.
Around the bend, new stories unfold,
In whispers warm, the magic's told.

The sky adorned in pastel hues,
Paints every path with dusky views.
In harmony, the world takes flight,
With every heartbeat, pure delight.

Among the ferns, where secrets nest,
The heart of spring knows no jest.
A vibrant brush, the wildflowers play,
In nature's arms, we dream away.

So listen close, to life's refrain,
In every drop of soft spring rain.
For tales and springs, hand in hand,
Compose the world's most wondrous band.

Dappled Light and Delighted Whispers

Through leafy canopies, sunlight streams,
Painting the earth with golden dreams.
Where shadows dance and spirits twine,
In dappled light, our hearts entwine.

The murmurs weave through tranquil trees,
Carried softly upon the breeze.
With gentle rustle, the leaves agree,
To share their secrets, wild and free.

Among the blooms, the laughter stirs,
Each petal, a smile, the world concurs.
In gardens rich with life's embrace,
We find our joy, our sacred place.

Adventurous whispers ride the air,
Echoing softly, here and there.
With each gentle sigh, we find relief,
In nature's tapestry, we seek belief.

So close your eyes, let magic near,
In dappled light, your path is clear.
Delighted whispers echo bright,
Inviting dreams in day's soft light.

Where Shadows Play on Water's Edge

In twilight's glow, the shadows glide,
Where starlit waters softly bide.
Reflections whisper tales of old,
As night unfolds its velvet fold.

The ripples dance, a ghost's embrace,
Each shimmering wave, a fleeting grace.
On banks of thought, in silence deep,
The secrets of the dark we keep.

A moonlit path through whispers grey,
Guides wandering hearts along the way.
With every splash, a promise made,
In stillness, dreams and fears cascade.

The nightingale sings her serenade,
In rhythmic notes, the dusk is laid.
The past and present sweetly blend,
On water's edge, we find our mend.

So linger long where shadows play,
And let your worries drift away.
For in the calm and quiet sheen,
Lives the heart of what could have been.

The Twinkling Soiree of Nature's Spirits

Beneath the stars, in evening's thrall,
Nature's spirits gather, enthralled.
A twinkling soiree, bright and bold,
Where stories weave, both new and old.

With laughter ringing through the trees,
And melodies that ride the breeze.
Each twinkling light, a spark divine,
Guides every heart to joy's design.

The fireflies dance, a fleeting show,
Their glimmers soft, a fairy glow.
In this embrace, the world feels right,
As magic twirls in gentle flight.

From dusk till dawn, the night won't cease,
In whispered prayers, we find our peace.
Together here, through glen and grove,
The spirits sing, and hearts will rove.

So heed the call of nature's cheer,
And let each moment draw you near.
In twinkling hope, be ever bold,
For life's sweet soiree is purest gold.

Journey of the Wooded Nymphs

In twilight's glow, they weave and dance,
Among the trees, they take their chance.
With laughter bright, they chase the light,
In shadows deep, they vanish from sight.

Their whispers echo through the glade,
In secrets shared, no fears displayed.
With every step on forest floor,
They sing of tales, of ancient lore.

Bound to the roots, where magic thrives,
In harmony, their spirit strives.
With every breath of scented pine,
They swirl like mist, so pure, divine.

They paint the leaves with hues of dreams,
In silver streams, the sunlight beams.
A unity that cannot break,
In nature's arms, no souls forsake.

So wander still, where nymphs reside,
In every glance, let joy abide.
For in their world of soft embrace,
We find our truths, our truest grace.

Laughter Carried by the Fall's Breeze

When autumn's breath begins to sing,
The laughter spreads on rippling wing.
Leaves of gold float through the air,
Whirling gently, a dance so rare.

With every gust, the children cheer,
As nature's jesters draw near.
The crunch of leaves beneath their feet,
A melody, a joyful beat.

Pumpkins grin with mischief bright,
As shadows lengthen, day turns night.
The crispness wraps like a warm embrace,
In laughter sweet, we find our place.

So let us chase what autumn gives,
In every chuckle, our spirit lives.
With friends around, no fear remains,
As laughter dances through the strains.

And as the seasons come and go,
We carry forth the autumn's glow.
In laughter's arms, our hearts will sway,
Forever young, in fall's ballet.

Dreamweavers in the Velvet Underbrush

In twilight's hush, they spin their dreams,
The dreamweavers, through silver streams.
With gentle hands, they stroke the night,
In velvet shadows, their magic ignites.

Soft whispers rise from mossy beds,
In secret realms where silence treads.
They craft their spells with blossoms fair,
In every thread, a world laid bare.

With starlit eyes, they gaze above,
In endless skies, their hearts do love.
For every dream, a story grows,
In whispered winds, their journey flows.

They gather light from moons aglow,
And weave the tales we long to know.
Through thorny paths and hidden glades,
Their artistry in twilight fades.

So when you tread on forest's floor,
Remember dreams are at your door.
In underbrush where shadows blend,
The dreamweavers always send.

The Flow of Time in a Sylvan Dream

In sylvan woods where time stands still,
Moments linger, they softly spill.
Each rustling leaf, each gentle stream,
A tapestry weaves through the dream.

Time dances slow in nature's hold,
Pristine and pure, as stories unfold.
With every breath, a journey starts,
In whispered woods, we find our hearts.

Seasons shift in graceful sway,
Sculpting time in their own way.
From dawn's first light to dusk's embrace,
The flow of time finds its own pace.

Among the trees, we lose our care,
In echoes low, our spirits share.
With nature's pulse, we learn to see,
The precious gift of what can be.

So linger here, let worries fade,
In sylvan sanctum gently laid.
For in the woods, as shadows gleam,
We flow with time in a timeless dream.

Fantasies in the Glittering Green

In the forest where shadows play,
Leaves whisper secrets, soft and gay.
Creatures dance in the light of the moon,
As dreams awaken, a gentle tune.

Winds weave through branches, a silver thread,
Crickets chirp as the daylight's shed.
Fairies sprinkle stardust in the night,
Filling the air with a magic sight.

Mossy stones cradle fairy's laughter,
While time slips by, with joy thereafter.
Each step reveals a hidden delight,
In dreams that shimmer, so pure and bright.

Moonbeams kiss the blossoms anew,
In this realm, all wishes come true.
A canvas painted in vibrant hue,
Where fantasies blossom like morning dew.

With every heartbeat, spirits soar,
In harmony with the forest's roar.
Unraveled mysteries wait to be found,
In the glittering green, bliss profound.

Glinting Ripples Beneath Giggles

By the brook where the children play,
Laughter dances in the light of day.
Ripples glint as they skip and dip,
While dreams sail on a sun-kissed trip.

Fluttering butterflies join the cheer,
As whispers of water sing sweetly near.
Pebbles shimmer with a joyful glow,
Each splash a secret, a tale to sow.

Sunlight weaves through the leaves above,
Creating a tapestry of nature's love.
The brook gurgles and giggles along,
Building a rhythm; a playful song.

Every moment flows like a gentle stream,
In a world that feels like a waking dream.
Where wonder rests beneath the bright skies,
And laughter twinkles in children's eyes.

In the glinting waters, magic blends,
An eternal play where the joy never ends.
With every droplet, new memories rise,
Beneath the surface, life's sweet surprise.

The Elf's Delight in Water's Flow

In the glades where the soft streams glide,
An elf sits quietly, magic as his guide.
With nimble fingers, he weaves a spell,
Crafting whispers that only the waters can tell.

Sunlight dances on rippling waves,
Reflecting stories that the water saves.
From crystal pools, ancient legends bloom,
Filling the air with an enchanting loom.

Lily pads float like boats on dreams,
While playful fish flicker in silver beams.
The elf delights in the songs they share,
In rhythms of nature, woven with care.

He gathers the essence of rain's sweet grace,
Capturing moments in this tranquil place.
Every droplet becomes a treasure rare,
In the flow of water, freedom and flair.

With joyful laughter, he twirls and spins,
Embracing the beauty where the river begins.
In this haven, his heart takes flight,
For the elf's delight lies in water's light.

The Harmony of Hidden Springs

In a meadow kissed by the morning sun,
Hidden springs whisper where shadows run.
Nature's lullaby guides the breeze,
Wrapping the world in sweet melodies.

Each ripple sings a tale of old,
Where secrets of earth and water unfold.
Moonlight dances as dusk draws near,
In the heart of the springs, all things are clear.

Birds take flight, their calls like chimes,
Echoing softly through ancient times.
Fauna gather, enchanted and free,
Under the dance of the willow tree.

In this sanctuary, life intertwines,
With every heartbeat, a story shines.
In the embrace of the hidden springs,
A harmony plays, where the spirit sings.

Here peace and joy forever remain,
Where whispers of laughter wash away pain.
Through each fleeting moment, hearts will find,
The magic in springs that truly bind.

The Lullaby of Ancient Trees

In the heart of the forest, whispers soft,
Leaves dance in the breeze, their spirits aloft.
Roots woven deep in the tales of the past,
Guardians of secrets, their shadows cast.

Branches embrace the starlit night,
Crickets sing gently, a soothing light.
Moonbeams filter through emerald lace,
In the arms of the trees, find your place.

Their bark tells stories of ages gone by,
Of storms they have weathered, and whispers on high.
Each ring a reminder of time's gentle flow,
In the lullaby sung, let your worries go.

Come lay by their trunks, let dreams take flight,
As the world fades away in the soft, silver light.
In the rustle of leaves, hear the sweet call,
Of the ancient trees, beloved by all.

So drift into slumber, let silence be heard,
In the cradle of nature, sleep undeterred.
With the forest watching, your dreams will take wing,
In the embrace of the trees, you'll find peace in the spring.

Undercurrents of Joy and Enchantment

In the quiet corners where laughter glows,
Life weaves a tapestry, magic flows.
With the flicker of light, and the gentle breeze,
Whispers of wonder dance through the trees.

In gardens of dreams, where secrets align,
Each petal a promise, each leaf a sign.
Nature's own symphony plays from the heart,
Undercurrents of joy, a delicate art.

With each passing moment, a spark ignites,
In the hush of dawn, in the starlit nights.
Chasing the shadows, we find little things,
In the depths of our souls, the enchantment sings.

With a flick of the wand, or a wink of an eye,
Adventure awaits, beneath the vast sky.
Join the dance of the fireflies' flight,
In the web of delight, lose yourself in the night.

So gather your hopes, let your spirit soar,
In the embrace of the world, discover much more.
For joy is the current that flows all around,
In the heart of the magic, true happiness found.

The Graceful Path of Water's Whisper

Through glades where sunlight weaves,
The water sings a soft refrain,
It dances on the petal leaves,
A gentle flow, a sweet champagne.

Each ripple tells a tale untold,
Of dreams that linger in the air,
As moonlight bathes the world in gold,
The silver brook begins to care.

The stones are whispers from the past,
They cradle secrets, old and wise,
In every glance, in every cast,
The water glimmers, truth belies.

With laughter bright and soft embrace,
It winds through valleys, rich and deep,
A sacred song, a timeless grace,
The path it charts, for souls to keep.

Beneath the bridge where lilies sigh,
The whispers turn to dreams anew,
In ripples where the wishes lie,
The water's path forever true.

Flickering Lights in the Woodland Veil

In hidden glades where shadows play,
The lights begin to twinkle bright,
As fireflies dance at close of day,
In magic swirls of soft twilight.

Each flicker weaves a tale at night,
A whisper shared with trees and moss,
They guide the wanderers' delight,
A luminescent, gentle gloss.

Through branches twisted, old and grand,
The glow entrusts its secret lore,
Inviting hearts with outstretched hand,
To wander paths unseen before.

The Woodland Veil, a quilt of dreams,
Embraces all in tender light,
Each flicker pulls at heartstrings' seams,
A dance of spirits through the night.

As dawn begins to paint the skies,
The lights retreat, yet dreams remain,
In every soul, a spark that flies,
With flickering hope, to start again.

Shadows Dancing by the Gentle Brook

Beneath the boughs of emerald green,
Where sunlight dapples on the ground,
The shadows dance, a subtle scene,
In rhythm with the brook's soft sound.

They sway in time with rustling leaves,
As whispers call from every nook,
The forest breathes, each heart believes,
In nature's song, the spirits look.

The brook reflects the fleeting day,
With silver glints and secrets shared,
In moments lost, they slip away,
Yet echo still, their whispers bared.

The world unfolds in twilight's hue,
As shadows weave their dance so near,
In every curve, a life renews,
With gentle flows, the past is clear.

As darkness falls, the tales abide,
In every shadow, stories brook,
The dancing forms, like dreams, reside,
Along the path where hope once took.

Playful Spirits Amongst the Bloom

In gardens bright with colors bold,
Where petals flutter in the breeze,
The playful spirits, young and old,
Dance joyfully among the trees.

They weave through blossoms, soft and light,
With laughter echoing through the air,
In sunlit fields, a wondrous sight,
Their magic thrives, a vital flair.

The daisies nod, and roses sway,
As spirits trace the scents they seek,
Each blossom joins the grand ballet,
In hues of joy, they softly speak.

The bumblebees hum sweetly near,
As petals blush, and life awakes,
In every bloom, a tale sincere,
A tapestry that nature makes.

As twilight wraps its silken thread,
The playful spirits softly fade,
Yet in each blossom, dreams are bred,
Amongst the bloom, their dance displayed.

Luminous Fables in a Whispering Wood

In the shadows where secrets lie,
Whispers of magic weave and fly.
Glimmers dance on leaves so bright,
Ancient tales come to light.

Creatures stir in twilight's breath,
Guardians of life, not of death.
With a flicker, stories start,
Each a thread, each a heart.

The brook sings with a gentle tune,
Softly kissed by the silver moon.
Echoes of laughter ring clear,
In this realm, all is dear.

Underneath the emerald boughs,
Mystics tread on time's soft vows.
A tapestry of dreams unfolds,
A legacy that never grows old.

Follow the path where shadows play,
In a dance of night and day.
For in this wood, magic thrives,
In luminous fables, life survives.

Tranquil Murmurs of Nature's Heart

In the hush of morning light,
Nature whispers, calm and bright.
Birds compose a lilting song,
Where the wildflowers belong.

Gentle breezes carry tales,
Of ancient trees and whispered gales.
Streams like silver ribbons weave,
Knitting dreams that never leave.

Each leaf dances in delight,
Filling souls with pure respite.
In the garden, time stands still,
Heartbeats echo, soft and shrill.

Mossy stones, a haven sweet,
Where all of nature's voices meet.
In this sanctuary, we abide,
With tranquil murmurs as our guide.

Awake, arise, the day begins,
With gentle grace, our spirit spins.
For in the heart of quiet hours,
Lies the magic of nature's powers.

Twilight's Embrace in a Mystic Grove

As daylight fades to dusky grey,
The whispering trees begin to sway.
In twilight's glow, all seems to dream,
A soft enchantment, a silken seam.

The stars emerge, a scattered light,
Guiding our hearts through the night.
Beneath the boughs so wise and old,
Secrets shimmer, stories told.

A gentle breeze hums a tune,
Crickets serenade the moon.
In this grove where shadows blend,
Time and reality softly mend.

With every rustle, nature sighs,
As fireflies dance in the mid-July.
Life intertwines in a sacred dance,
Inviting all to take a chance.

Let go of worries, breathe in deep,
In twilight's embrace, dreams softly creep.
For in this hour, magic glows,
In a mystic grove where the wonder flows.

Playful Spirits of the Woodland Realm

Among the trees, the spirits play,
In a lively, joyful ballet.
Twinkling eyes and laughter bright,
Filling the woods with pure delight.

With nimble feet and hearts so free,
They dance like whispers on the breeze.
Each leap a spark, each twirl a cheer,
Inviting all who wander near.

Mushrooms nod in merry glee,
As sunlight filters through each tree.
Beneath the boughs, enchantments thrive,
The woodland pulses, so alive.

With every rustle, joy ignites,
A symphony of woodland lights.
Where echoes of laughter remain,
In the rhythm of joy, no pain.

So roam the paths where spirits dwell,
In this realm where stories swell.
For in their mischief, hope will bloom,
Playful spirits dispel the gloom.

Whispers of Enchanted Streams

In the murmur of the brook, soft and clear,
Magical tales dance upon my ear.
Glimmers of starlight, the water's embrace,
Lead me to wonder, in this secret place.

Willows sway gently, their branches a sigh,
A world built of dreams beneath the vast sky.
Echoes of laughter, long vanished from view,
Where spirits once lingered, now spirits renew.

The stones are adorned with the wisdom of old,
Guardians of stories, in silence they hold.
Ripples of history, each course they chart,
In whispers of water, I find my lost heart.

By moonlit reflections, I wander and roam,
Finding my solace, the stream feels like home.
With a flick of their tails, the fish dance and play,
Inviting the night to join in their sway.

As dawn peeks through branches, the magic is spun,
The sunbeams break free, the night now is done.
Yet in dreams, I'll linger, where shadows still gleam,
Forever enchanted by the stream's gentle dream.

Meadow Melodies Under Moonlight

In the heart of the meadow, the magic unfolds,
Where echoes of starlight in silence are told.
Crickets compose while the fireflies dance,
Crafting sweet melodies, a marvelous chance.

Petals unfurl with the touch of the night,
A tapestry woven in shimmering light.
Each whisper of wind shares a secret or two,
As shadows pirouette in the midnight's blue.

Soft grasses sway to a lullaby's tune,
Beneath the soft glow of a silvery moon.
All creatures awaken, in harmony play,
The meadow breathes magic, at the end of the day.

With a sprinkle of stardust, the dreams come alive,
In this mystical realm, where wishes will thrive.
Every star a reminder, of hopes held so tight,
Under the canvas of this deep, velvet night.

As soft as the whispers that linger on air,
The meadow holds secrets, both precious and rare.
In the hush of the moonlight, I find my own song,
A symphony crafted, where all of us belong.

Laughter of the Forest Glade

Among the tall trees, where shadows do play,
The forest reveals its enchanting display.
Branches sway gently, a whimsical breeze,
Echoing laughter that dances with ease.

Sunlight weaves gold through the leaves overhead,
While creatures emerge from the warmth of their bed.
Squirrels chatter merrily, gnawing on treats,
While rabbits skip lightly on soft, mossy seats.

In the heart of the glade, where joy reigns supreme,
Nature sings freely, a jubilant dream.
A ripple of laughter, so tender and bright,
Binds every heart in this magical light.

With flowers in bloom and a soft, lilting sound,
The forest, it beckons, at joy's blessed ground.
Each moment a treasure, each sight a delight,
In laughter and wonder, the world feels so right.

Even as twilight begins its descent,
The laughter lingers; it's never quite spent.
For in every shadow, in each glimmered ray,
The heart of the forest is here to stay.

Secrets in the Twinkling Shadows

In the veil of dusk, where the shadows reside,
Whispers of magic in darkness abide.
Stars twinkle softly, a celestial guide,
Leading me deeper, where mysteries hide.

The rustle of leaves tells tales not yet heard,
Of creatures unseen, in the night, they are stirred.
While moonbeams weave softly through branches so high,

I wander in wonder, beneath the night sky.

Each flicker of light, a secret untold,
The night holds its stories in sparkles of gold.
The shadows, they beckon, with magic so rare,
Inviting the curious, inviting the dare.

A soft breeze carries the scent of the past,
As echoes of laughter in twilight are cast.
In the hush of the night, I can almost perceive,
The depth of the whispers that twilight does weave.

As dawn starts to rise, the secrets retreat,
Yet beneath the bright sky, their essence will meet.
In every soft shadow, a memory stays,
The magic of twilight will never fade away.

The Riddle of the Enchanted Ripples

In the brook where whispers play,
Silver gleams in disarray,
Secrets dance beneath the tide,
Mysteries the waters hide.

A woven tale of twilight's hue,
Echoes soft, a song so true,
Ripples weave a spellbound rhyme,
Calling forth the ancient time.

Gentle rush, a fleeting glance,
Frogs that leap in moonlit dance,
What is hidden, who will know?
Only those who search below.

A riddle wrapped in misty air,
To find the truth, they must dare,
Hear the call of water bright,
And follow shadows, kiss the night.

So tread with care along the stream,
Join the midnight's twisted dream,
For in the depths, the magic lives,
Where every drop a secret gives.

Blessed Ventures of the Woodland Dwellers

In the heart of ancient trees,
Whispered tales ride on the breeze,
Creatures small with hearts so bold,
Guard their treasures, worth more than gold.

Mushroom rings and faerie lights,
Glimmer softly through the nights,
Adventures loom beneath the leaves,
Where courage blooms, and joy believes.

Squirrels chatter, wise and spry,
Wielding acorns like a spy,
Each venture filled with playful schemes,
Unlocking all their woodland dreams.

In dappled shade, they gather near,
Sharing laughter, shedding fear,
Together strong, a merry band,
Crafting stories hand in hand.

For every path through forest wide,
Holds a secret, oh, what pride,
The woodland dwellers venture forth,
Cradling treasures of the earth.

Mirth in the Magical Murmurs

Beneath the boughs where shadows lie,
Laughter bubbles, soaring high,
Songs of sprites, a joyful feast,
In their realm, worries cease.

Glimpses of light, reflections swirl,
In this world, the magic unfurls,
Gentle whispers, tales anew,
Calling forth both me and you.

Dancing fairies, twirling round,
Joy is found in every sound,
Breezes carry echoes sweet,
Mirth and magic intertwine, complete.

In the stillness, hearts ignite,
Floating dreams take graceful flight,
With every twinkle in the air,
Miracles abound everywhere.

So heed the call of nature's song,
Join the laughter, it won't be long,
For in the woods, where spirits play,
Magic lives, come what may.

The Allure of the Forest's Edge

At the forest's edge, where shadows blend,
Curiosity and freedom send,
A world of wonders waits in line,
Enticing all with secrets divine.

Sunlight spills through branches wide,
Painting paths where dreams can hide,
Every rustling leaf insists,
Adventure calls through twilight mist.

A gentle sigh, a rustle near,
Through tangled roots, the way is clear,
Each step whispers, tales long spun,
Drawing out the heart of fun.

The allure of the wild is strong,
For every creature sings its song,
Together here, with lives entwined,
Embrace the magic, seek and find.

So come alive where echoes dwell,
Discover all the woods can tell,
For at the edge, the world's a stage,
With every breath, turn a new page.

Starlit Paths through Fabled Realms

Through whispering woods and shadows deep,
Where ancient secrets softly creep,
Footsteps lead on, where dreams reside,
On starlit paths, our hearts confide.

The nightingale sings, the moonlight glows,
In woven tales, the magic flows,
Each twinkle beckons, a silent call,
Illuminating wonders for one and all.

With every step, the air grows sweet,
The spirits dance in rhythms fleet,
We wander where the brave have trod,
In realms enchanted, blessed by God.

Here dragons soar and mermaids sway,
In twilight's grasp, night turns to day,
Through fabled realms, we're bound to roam,
In starlit paths, we find our home.

So take my hand, let's journey wide,
Where legend meets with time and tide,
Through whispered winds and ancients' sighs,
In magic's heart, our spirit flies.

Hidden Glimmers of Elven Delight

In the forest where the sunlight fades,
Glimmers dance like soft cascades,
Elven laughter fills the air,
A world of wonder, rich and rare.

Amongst the blooms where fairies play,
Secrets hide in hues of gray,
With every petal, stories spun,
Of twilight's grace and days undone.

With silken threads in twilight's charm,
The elven folk weave dreams, disarm,
Their gentle whispers call to thee,
In hidden glades, we long to be.

Crystal streams reflect the stars,
Guiding hearts from near and far,
In every flicker, hope takes flight,
In hidden glimmers, pure delight.

So follow me to realms untold,
Where every moment turns to gold,
In elven glades, let spirits twine,
In hidden joy, our hearts align.

The Dance of Water and Light

Beneath the waves, a whisper glows,
A fluid dance where magic flows,
With every ripple, a secret revealed,
In harmony, our fates are sealed.

The sunbeams waltz on water's face,
Creating ripples of sheer grace,
Each drop a diamond, glinting bright,
In the dance of water and light.

Together they twirl, weave, and spin,
As shadows play, and day begins,
An endless rhythm, a sacred bond,
In nature's heart, we journey on.

From babbling brooks to oceans wide,
The elements meet, side by side,
Through liquid mirrors, dreams ignite,
In the dance of water and light.

So let us lose ourselves tonight,
In this sweet dance, both pure and bright,
With open hearts, we take our flight,
In harmony's embrace, pure delight.

Reverie Beneath the Ancient Boughs

Beneath the boughs where shadows sigh,
In twilight's glow, the dreams drift by,
Among the roots, the stories dwell,
In whispers soft, they weave their spell.

The ancients watch with patient eyes,
Guarding secrets, silent ties,
Each branch a keeper of days gone past,
In reverie, our hearts hold fast.

The cool earth cradles thoughts anew,
As time slips by like morning dew,
In every leaf, a tale unfolds,
A tapestry of lives retold.

So let us wander, hand in hand,
In enchanted realms, we make our stand,
For beneath the boughs, our spirits soar,
In reverie, we seek for more.

In the hush of night, our voices blend,
With ancient whispers, we comprehend,
Beneath the boughs, where dreams take flight,
In sacred stillness, we find the light.

Tantalizing Currents of Whimsical Breezes

In secret glades where breezes play,
The whispers twist in charming sway.
Each leaf a dancer in the light,
They frolic softly, day to night.

With every gust, the stories flow,
Of ancient woods and tales we know.
They beckon forth with teasing grace,
To join the dance at Nature's pace.

A ribboned trail of scents so sweet,
Where dreams and laughter softly meet.
The sunbeams' waltz upon the stream,
Awakens all, igniting dreams.

When twilight drapes in hues of gold,
The breeze around our hearts enfolds.
A symphony of nightingale,
Each note a tale we long to hail.

So come, dear friend, with open eyes,
Embrace the breeze that softly sighs.
For in its song, a world awaits,
Where time dissolves, and fate creates.

The Pint-sized Parliament of Elves

In shadowed groves where laughter rings,
The elf folk gather, sprightly beings.
With tiny hats and twinkling eyes,
They scheme and plot 'neath starlit skies.

Around a stump, their council meets,
With acorns piled as tiny seats.
Their voices rise in merry cheer,
Decisions made on frothy beer.

With nimble hands and quickened feet,
They dance and spin to nature's beat.
Each elf a keeper of the lore,
They whisper tales from times of yore.

Their antics fill the night with glee,
As moonlight weaves through every tree.
A pint-sized realm of mischief bright,
Where every heart is pure delight.

So tread with care in woods so deep,
For if you pause, you just might see
The parliament, so sly and clever,
Working wonders, now and forever.

The Light and Life of Woodland Waters

Through shaded paths, the waters gleam,
Reflecting skies in silver beams.
The ripples sing of joy and plight,
As life awakens, pure and bright.

Where creatures sip and shadows dance,
The woodland holds a sacred trance.
Each droplet's shimmer, a tale to tell,
Of rising tides and secrets dwell.

The willows nod in gentle streams,
While fish below weave in their dreams.
The echoes rise, a chorus bold,
Of ancient tales that time has told.

With every glide and quiet sigh,
The waters weave their lullaby.
A canvas vast by Nature cast,
With every ripple, shadows past.

So linger near the woodland's flow,
Where life and light in harmony glow.
For in its depths, we find our place,
In every tear, a warm embrace.

Glistening Tales of Forest Joy

Beneath the boughs, where sunbeams play,
The forest sings in bright array.
With every step, a magic stirs,
Whispers of peace, as joy occurs.

The mushrooms bloom, a rainbow spread,
While fluttering faeries dance ahead.
Each rustling leaf tells tales anew,
Of glistening nights and skies so blue.

Upon the trail, where stories weave,
The laughter lingers, we believe.
With woven crowns of petals pure,
The joy of nature, sweet and sure.

The streams that gurgle, clear and bright,
Reflect the stars that pierce the night.
A serenade of sounds so dear,
Where life ignites and hearts draw near.

So wander wide, with open heart,
In every glance, a work of art.
For in the forest's tender grace,
We find our joy, our sacred space.

A Melody of Secrets and Sprites

In a glen where shadows play,
Whispers twine in soft ballet,
Moonlight weaves a silver thread,
Harmonies of dreams once said.

Flickering lights like fireflies,
Dancing gently through the skies,
Melodies of starlit nights,
Echo deep in heart's delights.

Secrets flutter on the breeze,
Wrapped in rustling autumn leaves,
Every sound a story spun,
Only shared with moon and sun.

Sprites in laughter, hearts aglow,
Guiding lost ones where to go,
Through the thicket, paths unknown,
In the realm where time has flown.

Listen close, the forest calls,
In its arms, a magic sprawls,
With each note, a spell is cast,
Moments cherished, ever vast.

Verdant Valleys and Dancing Lights

In verdant valleys, flowers bloom,
Underneath the twilight's gloom,
Colors whisper, lush and bright,
Nature's canvas, pure delight.

Golden sunbeams warmly spill,
Over mountains, soft and still,
Dancing lights in gentle breeze,
Swirling dreams among the trees.

Streams of silver, softly flow,
Mirror skies with hues aglow,
Nature's symphony unfolds,
Stories of the earth retold.

Creatures dwell in harmony,
Sharing secrets, wild and free,
Underneath the starlit dome,
In this valley, hearts find home.

Evenings wrapped in shadow's peace,
Moments linger, never cease,
In this realm of light and shade,
Eternal wonders never fade.

Celestial Reflections in Nature's Embrace

Beneath the sky's vast tapestry,
Where stars align in reverie,
Nature holds the secrets tight,
Celestial whispers through the night.

Mountains rise with silent grace,
Carved by time's relentless pace,
In each crevice, stories hide,
Of ancient spirits, side by side.

Rippling waters catch the glow,
Of countless stars that ebb and flow,
Moonlit paths lead dreams anew,
In reflections, hearts break through.

Gentle winds caress the leaves,
Tales of time that nature weaves,
With every rustle, nature sighs,
In its breath, eternity lies.

In this dance of night and day,
Life unfolds in sweet array,
Celestial wonders, embrace wide,
In nature's heart, our souls confide.

Tides of Time in the Fairy Realm

In the fairy realm where time bends,
Whispers of old stories blend,
With the glow of twilight's grace,
Magic lingers in this place.

Tides of time come and recede,
Carrying wishes, heart's deep need,
With each wave, a dream unleashed,
In this world, the soul is feasted.

Glimmers spark where fey reside,
In their laughter, secrets hide,
Every flower, every stone,
Holds the essence of the unknown.

Underneath the moon's soft glow,
Dancing winds begin to flow,
Guiding spirits in their flight,
Bringing forth enchantment's light.

In the shadows, magic weaves,
Eternity that never leaves,
Here in this realm, forever twine,
Tides of time, both yours and mine.

Elven Footprints on Fern-Laden Trails

In the glade where whispers play,
Elven feet leave prints of light.
Fern fronds dance in soft ballet,
Guided by the moonlit night.

Gentle breezes weave their spell,
Through the boughs with magic glows.
Ancient secrets, none can tell,
These are paths that dreamers know.

Mossy carpets cradle dreams,
Underneath the ancient oak.
Rippling like the silver streams,
Where the heart of nature spoke.

Softly now the twilight gleams,
As the stars begin to peep.
In the hush, the forest seems,
To hold tales that shadows keep.

With each step, a tale unfolds,
Echoing in twilight's grace.
In the trails where magic molds,
Elven secrets find their place.

Enigmas of the Faerie-Touched Glens

Beyond the hills where secrets lie,
Faerie whispers drift like mist.
In glens where shadows throng and sigh,
Mysteries awaken, soft and kissed.

The blooms hold tales of yesteryear,
Nestled in the emerald grass.
In every petal, joy and fear,
A moment's glance, the faeries pass.

Curled ferns embrace the silent ground,
While twilight dances in the air.
A hidden world, where dreams abound,
Is crafted in the night so fair.

Order of the nightingale's song,
Guides the lost through wooded ways.
In faerie glens, we all belong,
To a realm of wonder, a place to gaze.

Enigmas sway on twilight's breath,
Beneath the stars, in whispers deep.
Tracing paths that dance with death,
In faerie realms, our secrets keep.

A Tapestry of Tints in the Enchanted Canopy

Above, a canopy of dreams,
Woven bright with shades of gold.
Sunlight spills in glistening streams,
Where stories of the ancients unfold.

Crimson leaves like little flames,
Whisper tales of autumn's kiss.
Each hue a note in nature's games,
A symphony of peace, pure bliss.

Below, the carpet soft and green,
Cradles every footstep light.
In the light, colors intermingle,
Crafting day from the fabric of night.

As shadows play in gentle hues,
And sunlight dapples the cool earth,
Nature sings in vibrant news,
Celebrating every birth.

An artist's brush paints the sky,
In every breeze, a stroke displayed.
In this tapestry, wonders lie,
In enchanted woods, forever swayed.

Whirls of Wonder in the Shimmering Grove

In groves where light and shadow weave,
Whirls of wonder twirl and spin.
Flickering shapes, elusive thieves,
Capture moments where dreams begin.

The silken touch of dewdrop dreams,
Adorn the leaves in morning's light.
Whispers echo in silver streams,
Nature dances in pure delight.

Beneath the boughs, magic thrums,
With hidden rhythms in the air.
Where every step, adventure comes,
In a grove where marvels share.

Through tangled roots and fragrant thyme,
Life unfolds in vibrant shades.
Each heartbeat sings, a lyric rhyme,
In the heart of the glade, unafraid.

As stars emerge and shadows creep,
The grove transforms with twilight's kiss.
In whirls of wonder, the night shall keep,
The glow of magic, and timeless bliss.

Echoes of Enchantment Amidst the Pines

In the hush of the forest, whispers flow,
Magic weaves through each shadowed row.
Tall pines sway with a gentle grace,
Echoes of wonder embrace this place.

Moonlight dances on leaves so bright,
Filling the night with a soft silver light.
Creatures stir in the cool evening air,
Revealing secrets beyond compare.

In the heart where the wildflowers bloom,
Dreams intertwine, dispelling the gloom.
Nature's symphony calls out to all,
Silent enchantments in the night enthrall.

Winding paths lead to realms most rare,
Where time stands still in the fragrant air.
Mysterious echoes call to the wise,
Beneath starlit skies, the heart complies.

Moccasins and Moonbeams

Soft moccasins tread on the dew-kissed grass,
Guided by moonbeams as shadows pass.
Each step whispers tales of those who roam,
In the magic of night, we find our home.

Underneath the vast celestial dome,
Starlight sparkles, a path we comb.
With every heartbeat, a story unfolds,
In the warmth of the night, our adventure holds.

Gentle breezes carry laughter near,
Ghosts of the past, we hold dear.
Under the moon, we dance and twirl,
In the embrace of night, our dreams unfurl.

In harmony, our spirits sing,
Nature rejoices, and the heart takes wing.
Echoes of laughter blend with the trees,
As we wander on paths that weave with ease.

A Journey Through Sparkling Swirls

Step by step, we glide through the mist,
With sparkling swirls, the world can't resist.
Colors collide in the shimmering air,
Each moment breathes magic, beyond compare.

Beyond the horizon, where dreams take flight,
In a dance of wonder, we bask in the light.
Every corner reveals a tale anew,
Where fantasies linger, waiting for you.

Time feels enchanted, a delicate thread,
Connecting our hearts as we leap ahead.
Through glimmers and sparkles, we journey on,
In a land where the dusk turns to dawn.

With laughter bubbling like a mountain stream,
Amidst the swirls, we dare to dream.
Each step is laden with stories to tell,
Of magic and wonder, we know so well.

Harmony in the Elven Grove

In the heart of the grove, a melody stirs,
With whispers of magic that gently occurs.
Elven songs float on the breath of the trees,
Carried by breezes that dance with such ease.

Beneath the canopies, shadows entwine,
Illuminated softly, a divine design.
Every leaf holds a tale in its veins,
Echoing laughter, harmony reigns.

A tapestry woven of sights and sounds,
In this sacred place, forever it bounds.
Glistening flowers bloom in the light,
An ode to the reverie that fills the night.

With stars as our witnesses, we gather near,
In each others' gaze, there's no space for fear.
Embraced by the magic that lingers above,
We celebrate life in the Elven Grove.

The Dance of Hidden Glades

In silent woods where shadows play,
The whispers of the trees sway,
A dance unfolds, both light and free,
Among the glades, just you and me.

The flickering fireflies take their flight,
In twinkling paths, they spark the night,
With every step, the earth will hum,
To nature's song, we leap and come.

The velvet moss beneath our toes,
In gentle breezes, magic grows,
As moonbeams cast their silver thread,
We weave our dreams where spirits tread.

With laughter shared and hearts ablaze,
We chase the stars through mystic haze,
In hidden glades where time stands still,
Our dance a promise, deep and thrill.

When dawn breaks softly on our way,
We'll part but carry night's ballet,
For in the woods, our souls will stay,
In whispered glades, forever play.

Secrets Among the Ferns

Beneath the ferns in shadows deep,
The secrets of the wild we keep,
In every rustle, tales unfold,
Of ancient trees and whispers bold.

The sunlight filters like a dream,
Amongst the roots, we softly gleam,
In hidden corners, stories pause,
To share with us their ancient laws.

With tender touch, we trace the leaves,
As nature spins her webs and weaves,
A tapestry of green and gold,
Where every burrow hides a hold.

Join hands with me, embrace the hush,
Through tranquil paths, we'll gently rush,
In every footprint, echoes stay,
As secrets weave along our way.

When twilight falls and shadows merge,
In fern-clad glades, our spirits surge,
For in the heart of every fern,
Lies wisdom waiting for our turn.

Laughter in the Leafy Canopy

In leafy heights where laughter sings,
The canopy hides such joyous flings,
With chirping birds, the day is bright,
As whispers of green dance in light.

Above the world, we toss and play,
On branches strong, we find our way,
In nature's court, we jest and climb,
Each moment felt, a willful rhyme.

The rustling leaves, a playful tune,
Under the watch of afternoon,
In sunlit gaps, our shadows lean,
Our laughter spills, a vibrant sheen.

Let's twirl with joy, forget the grind,
In leafy laughter, lose all bind,
For in the canopy's warm embrace,
We find the world, a cherished place.

As day gives way to evening's glow,
In echoes soft, our breezes flow,
In leafy joy, our hearts extend,
With laughter shared, our souls unbend.

Glittering Waters Under Moonlight

Beneath the cloak of silver night,
The waters shimmer, pure and bright,
In moonlit pools, reflections dance,
A magical invitation to chance.

The ripples sing, a soft embrace,
Where stars above find their place,
In tranquil depths, the world will fade,
A perfect dream in twilight laid.

We wander near the water's edge,
With whispers low, we take a pledge,
To cherish each moment held so dear,
As moonlit dreams draw us near.

The silver path unfolds with grace,
Inviting us to a gentle space,
Our laughter mingles with the stream,
As time dissolves in night's soft dream.

And when the dawn calls us to rise,
We'll carry forth the moonlit ties,
For in the waters, hearts have met,
In glittering dreams, we won't forget.

Moonlit Waves and Woodland Glimmers

Beneath the moon's soft, silver glow,
The waves whisper secrets, ebb and flow.
In wooded realms where shadows play,
Mysteries linger at the end of day.

The nightingale sings a lullaby sweet,
While starlit paths invite our feet.
Each wave a dancer, each glimmer a star,
Together they weave dreams from afar.

The forest breathes in the cool night air,
As moonbeams glisten on mossy lair.
A quiet magic, profound and deep,
Lulls the weary world into sleep.

In twilight's grasp, all is tranquil and still,
A silvered embrace, a gentle thrill.
As waves crash softly on the moonlit sands,
Nature's enchantment, it tenderly stands.

So wander here where the shadows bend,
Embrace the night, let your spirit blend.
For in this realm of waves and trees,
The heart finds solace, the soul hears ease.

Secrets of Laughter Drift

In hidden glades where laughter lies,
Secrets dance beneath bright skies.
Whispers of joy float through the air,
Crafting memories, light as a feather.

The playful breeze, a cheeky sprite,
Tickles the leaves, ignites delight.
Laughter echoes in every nook,
A cheerful melody, a storybook.

Sunlight dapples through branches above,
Painting the world in hues of love.
Each giggle, a spark that ignites the day,
Chasing the shadows, keeping gloom at bay.

In the arms of nature's warm embrace,
Every smile blooms, every heart finds place.
And as the day starts to gently fade,
The secrets of laughter will never degrade.

So let your spirit take to the sky,
With every chuckle, let your heart fly.
For in this world where joy takes flight,
The secrets of laughter are pure delight.

Celestial Dances of the Serene Stream

Upon the banks where the waters gleam,
Dreams take shape in a gentle stream.
Each ripple whispers a soft refrain,
Tales of starlight and moonlit rain.

The cosmos twirls in a silvery hue,
As night unfolds, painting skies anew.
Fish leap freely in a joyous spree,
Reflecting the dance of eternity.

With each soft murmur, the current tells,
Of enchanted lands and magical spells.
In this serene ballet, hopes take flight,
Adrift in the arms of the tranquil night.

Stars glitter bright, a twinkling throng,
Guiding the water's melodic song.
Where dreams and reflections intertwine,
In celestial dances, fate is divine.

So follow the path where the waters wind,
In the heart of the night, solace you'll find.
For in this blissful, serene stream's glow,
The secrets of the cosmos gently flow.

The Gesang of Glimmering Groves

In glimmering groves where fairies weave,
Nature sings, an enchanting reprieve.
With every leaf, a story is sown,
In rustling whispers, life is grown.

The night air hums a symphony sweet,
As shadows sway in the moon's heartbeat.
A tapestry woven with starlight's thread,
Where dreams awaken and fears are shed.

Branches above sway in graceful delight,
Guiding lost souls through the hush of night.
In the glow of the moon, hearts start to soar,
As the gesang calls, we yearn for more.

Every flicker, a promise, a spark,
Illuminating paths through the dark.
In the hidden alcoves, magic ignites,
Creating a world where the brave take flight.

So linger here in the groves' embrace,
Let the whispering winds quicken your pace.
For in the glimmering twilight's lace,
The songs of the woods reveal their grace.

The Elves' Serenade at Twilight

In twilight's glow, the elves take flight,
With silver wings that shimmer bright.
They dance on whispers, soft and low,
In harmony with the stars' soft glow.

Their laughter twinkles through the trees,
A melody carried by the breeze.
With every note, the shadows sigh,
As night unfurls its velvet sky.

The moonbeams waltz, the fireflies play,
In magic's grip, the world gives way.
The ancient oaks sway to the song,
Where dreamers and elves both belong.

Through tangled vines and mossy paths,
Their serenade brings joy and laughs.
In every heart, a spark ignites,
Under the gaze of the starlit nights.

So linger near when twilight calls,
And let the elven magic enthrall.
For in their song, our hopes align,
In the timeless dance of the divine.

Mystical Currents of the Starlit Grove

In a grove where shadows weave,
The starlit night begins to breathe.
Mysterious currents flow like streams,
Carrying whispers of ancient dreams.

The leaves rustle soft as secrets told,
Beneath the trees, both thick and old.
With roots entwined, they share their lore,
Of magic woven forevermore.

The moonlight glimmers on the brook,
As sylvan creatures pause to look.
With every ripple, a tale unfolds,
Of fables and wonders, both bold and old.

In shadows deep, a flicker bright,
A promise held in the heart of night.
The current hums a silent call,
In the starlit grove, we are one and all.

So listen close, and you may find,
The secrets held in the night winds' kind.
In mystical currents, our souls shall play,
Guided by stars till the break of day.

Fables of the Forest Stream

Beside the stream, where water gleams,
Fables whisper in silver dreams.
The forest shares its stories old,
In rippling tones, like treasures told.

A turtle slow, a fox so spry,
Each creature adds its gentle sigh.
From willow's shade, wise owls do hoot,
In every corner, a tale takes root.

Time dances lightly on grassy knolls,
Every ripple cradles lost souls.
With laughter echoing in the trees,
The forest's heart begins to tease.

In the soft light, dreams slowly bloom,
Lighting the path as shadows loom.
For every tale of love or strife,
Flows through the stream, the pulse of life.

So wander here, let stories flow,
In fables found where wildflowers grow.
And listen well, for once you hear,
The stream's sweet song will draw you near.

Joyful Ripples in a Forgotten Valley

In a valley where the wildflowers sway,
Joyful ripples chase shadows away.
The air is thick with laughter and light,
As sunbeams pour in, making all bright.

A babbling brook sings a merry tune,
As butterflies dance under the moon.
Each petal shines, a burst of cheer,
In this forgotten place, magic draws near.

Bright-eyed creatures lift their heads high,
To watch as the clouds drift lazily by.
In harmony with the gentle breeze,
Life flourishes under emerald trees.

The valley whispers secrets soft,
In the tender glow of evening's croft.
With every ripple, a promise is spun,
Of joy that lingers till day is done.

So wander here where the heart feels free,
In joyful ripples, let your spirit be.
For in this valley, lost yet found,
A tapestry of happiness abounds.

Echoes of Treetop Harmony

In the haven where the leaves sway,
Whispers dance with the sun's warm rays.
Branches cradle songs of the breeze,
Nature hums in tranquil ease.

Each flicker of light tells a tale,
Of woodland spirits who never pale.
With echoes soft as a lover's sigh,
They weave the dreams that never die.

From flowers bright to skies of blue,
The forest breathes life, ever new.
In shadows cast by ancient trees,
Our hearts find peace as we believe.

So linger here, let worries slide,
In harmony where wonders bide.
The treetops hold a sacred space,
A realm where love has found its place.

Glimmers of Joy Beneath the Boughs

Beneath the boughs, where laughter lies,
Glimmers of joy dance in the skies.
With petals golden, they gently fall,
Nature's laughter, a wondrous call.

The brook sings sweet with a sparkling tune,
As dragonflies twirl 'neath the crescent moon.
In every ripple, a secret shared,
In this hidden glen, none are spared.

The air is thick with magic's thread,
Where dreams take flight, and fears are shed.
Beneath great oaks, we weave our plans,
In this green kingdom, united we stand.

The sunlight dances on leaves above,
Each shimmer a blessing, a sign of love.
Here in the wild, we find our worth,
Glimmers of joy, our souls' rebirth.

Enchanted Waters and Whimsy Whispers

In enchanted waters, secrets flow,
Rippling softly, a world aglow.
Whimsy whispers on the breeze,
With tales of wonder that drift with ease.

The willow weeps with grace divine,
While fireflies dance on the silvery line.
Each splash, a laughter, each wave, a sigh,
The heart swells wide as dreams flutter by.

A pixie's giggle, a soft delight,
Guides lost souls through the velvet night.
Listen closely, the waters speak,
Of ancient quests that still seek.

So dip your toes in the magic here,
Let whispers of whimsy draw you near.
For in every current, hope resides,
In enchanted waters, our spirit abides.

The Frolic of Nymphs in the Glade

In the heart of the glade, where shadows play,
Nymphs frolic softly in the light of day.
With laughter bright and voices clear,
They weave a spell that draws us near.

Dressed in petals, adorned with dew,
They dance in circles, a vibrant view.
Each twirl a tale, each leap a dream,
In this sacred grove, all is as it seems.

The woodland hums with a vibrant song,
As nature joins them, where we belong.
The breeze carries secrets, sweet and mild,
In the frolic of nymphs, we're all beguiled.

So come, dear wanderer, take their hand,
In the cadence of joy, together we stand.
For in this glade, where enchantments twine,
The frolic of nymphs, a dance divine.